THE QUICK START GUIDE

SPEAK UP! AND SUCCEED

Nance Rosen

The Quick Start Guide SPEAK UP! & SUCCEED

How to get everything you want in meetings, presentations and conversations

First Edition

Pegasus Media World • Beverly Hills, California

Pegasus Media World
PO Box 7816
Beverly Hills, CA 90212
orders@pegasusmediaworld.com
http://PegasusMediaWorld.com
www.NanceSpeaks.com

The Quick Start Guide
Speak Up! and Succeed
How to Get Everything You Want in Meetings, Presentations and Conversations

ISBN, print ed. 978-0-9786078-9-0
ISBN, PDF ed. 978-0-9786078-8-3
ISBN, Audio ed. 978-0-9786078-7-6
ISBN, LIT ed. 978-0-9786078-6-9

Library of Congress Catalog Card Number: 2007932544
Rosen, Nance.
The quick start guide: speak up! and succeed, how to get everything you want in meetings, presentations and conversations/Nance Rosen
1st ed.
ISBN0-9786078-1-3
1. Business 2. Sales 3. Motivation 4. Leadership

Edited by
Marianne D. Wallace
Lauraine Gustafson

First Printing 2007

Unattributed quotations are by Nance Rosen. Anecdotes and profiles of well-known individuals cited are true to the best knowledge of the author at this time. In keeping with the HBR case approach, examples contained within the writing reflect actual and common communication and managerial challenges and offer direct expressions of effective solutions, while the names of the speakers and companies along with certain details have been fictionalized where necessary to protect their identities.

Table of Contents

About the Author

Nance Rosen, MBA, is the managing partner of NAX Partners, a marketing and communications consulting company. She is also a professor of marketing at UCLA Business and Management in the continuing executive education program.

She speaks around the world to audiences on business communication, consumer buying behavior, sales, marketing and customer satisfaction. She also facilitates employee satisfaction and sensitivity programs and coaches managers and entrepreneurs on leading their organizations. She trains sales representatives, engineers, crew members and others who interact with buyers.

Formerly, Nance was a marketing executive at The Coca-Cola Company, president of the Medical Marketing Association, first woman director of marketing in the Fortune 500 technology sector, host of *International Business* on public radio, an entrepreneur and a general manager at Bozell Advertising and Public Relations (now Omnicom).

Her new book, *Speak Up! and Succeed: How to Get Everything You Want in Meetings, Presentations and Conversations*, springs forth from her rich background, offering readers access to her vast experience, intimate knowledge of the ins and outs of marketing and communication and her in-the-trenches understanding of how people work. As supplements to *Speak Up! and Succeed*, Nance is also offering the *Speak Up! and Succeed Quick Start Guide*, workbooks, e-books and multimedia presentations.

Be sure to check out www.NanceSpeaks.com for a wealth of additional information and resources. Meeting planners may be interested in her business communications packages, including customized keynotes, seminars and workshops plus materials and web content for association meetings or corporate audiences, including your sales force, technical staff, company employees, project teams and senior executives. For information about training, visit www.NanceSpeaks.com.

Nance's firm, NAX Partners, produces research and analysis on new markets and product portfolio expansion; a full range of communications including Web sites, brochures, advertising, sales support, seminars, events and marketing programs; and employee training programs along with other human resources support. For more information, visit www.NAXpartners.com.

You may reach Nance by calling 1-888-GO NANCE or via e-mail at Nance@NanceRosen.com. Mail may be sent to Nance Rosen, PO Box 7816, Beverly Hills, CA 90212.

Introduction

WHAT ARE YOU waiting for?

Whatever you want is out there, waiting for you to come and get it.

To speed you along your path to success, I've created this quick start guide to the Speak Up System.

This system is all about your getting exactly what you want as rapidly as humanly possible. I stress the human part, because success is a two-part equation, with both parts involving humans. Part one is about *you* and you alone. You must do your best as you produce the stuff of work: reports, bids, spreadsheets, designs, programs and the like. I'm counting on that.

Part two of the success equation is all about how you deal with other people. How good are you at getting other people to do what you want?

Do you fully understand the role of these other people? They can say "yes," produce what you need, agree to the schedule you want, write the check and go above and beyond their job descriptions. In a thousand different ways they can accelerate your progress and speed up your journey to success. You cannot succeed without them, and you will not get to enjoy the wildly happy and satisfied life you deserve unless they feel driven to help you along your path. That's what this book is about.

I wrote this book because after years in business in some of the world's largest companies, including The Coca-Cola Company, and in some lesser-known organizations, including The Medical Marketing Association, I had to leave the work world. To most people, it seemed that I left for great opportunities in media and academia, but I really had to leave business and industry for one reason: I had to get a grip on why everyone was so miserable at work. From almost everyone I spoke with—in my organization, at industry gatherings, sitting next to strangers on airplanes, at dinner with friends—one refrain kept being repeated. People complained about other people. It seemed that almost everyone was frustrated, depressed, angry and disturbed about the same thing: other people.

The stories varied, but the theme was the same. It could be the jerk they worked for, the lazy co-workers they dealt with, the stalling customers who wouldn't sign orders or the investors and bankers who wouldn't fund deals. I never heard anyone joyfully recounting a great conversation, presentation or meeting at work.

I knew plenty of successful people, but they were suffering for that success. They were muscling their way to the top and they were showing the signs of all that stress. I did, too. My career was like a speeding bullet. I ran a major division for one of the top two ad agencies in the US by the time I was twenty-five. I was a director of marketing in the Fortune 500 at the age of twenty-eight. I was president of a trade association at thirty-two. I ran my own consulting firm for ten years, during which time we won seventy-nine percent of all of the business pitches we made. I sat on the boards of several companies. I certainly enjoyed interacting with the incredibly talented, wise and decent people I met during all those years, but after being courted and employed by the number one most recognized brand in the world, I left the business world—to everyone's surprise.

Like a professional athlete seriously injured from years in the game, I was exhausted and in pain after all my "success."

So, I took what I planned would be one year off from the fast track and got a job hosting a program called *International Business* on public radio. I did it for ten years, added a syndicated television program called *NightCap* for a couple of years and began teaching executives, engineers and managers who were continuing their education on the campuses of UCLA and the University of California, Irvine. These students then hired me to train their people on marketing, sales, negotiations, product development and leadership, and, with my incredible staff at NAX Partners, produce marketing and communications programs.

Their invitations took me around the world, and brought the world to me. I now have thousands of alumni in about forty countries. I serve large and small companies, governments, trade and business associations and conduct summits with communications training and marketing programs.

After this decade of teaching, training and consulting, it became apparent to me that most individuals and their organizations believe they aren't good enough at the thing they do. Is there something wrong with their marketing and sales strategy? Product development platforms or quality? Customer service? Employee retention and satisfaction programs?

Yes, sometimes there are deficiencies in products, programs and plans. But, they are very easy to see and the fixes are not all that hard to implement. In fact, the bigger the problem in any of these areas, the more obvious and satisfying the solution.

However, even when they make the change in systems, procedures and products, almost every one of these individuals and companies doesn't get all the success they could enjoy. Why? It is because action—making better products, producing better reports, understanding and targeting the market better and managing their finances—is only half of the equation for success.

The second half of the success equation is interaction: what people do when they are in front of their prospects, customers, superiors, subordinates, suppliers, strategic partners, investors and other key influencers. How well they communicate—or fail to communicate—determines whether others will take action or not.

In most business situations, you can only succeed through speed. Competition sees the same opportunities you do. All products and services can be copied, and with a bigger marketing effort or more sales feet on the street, your competition can overtake you. That is, if you are only focused on your features, functions, policy and strategy—your stuff.

If you are better at getting people to take action, then you are going to be more successful more quickly than anyone else. Wielding the weapon of speed gets you to the highest ground, where you can see most choices. Then you have a lot of control over what you do and how much compensation and recognition you get.

It doesn't matter what you do for a living, success is always going to depend on your having a reliable method for getting others to do things your way, to approve the projects and plans you desire, to say "yes" when you can't afford a "no."

That's why I wrote this book. I looked at thousands of individuals and their interactions at work. I picked the ones that were most instructive, both for what they did right and what they did wrong. Then I applied the classical literature on consumer buying behavior, including my own findings in this academic and applied discipline. Finally, I developed a method that I call the Speak Up System. It's easy to use and effective no matter what type of interaction you have. It's been tested and approved by sales representatives, engineers, managers at all levels, trainers, professionals and business owners, from veterans to newbies. After five years of refining it on the road, I put the highlights of the system into this quick start guide.

So, you and I are going on this journey to your success. It is my most ardent desire that you find work satisfying in all the big and small ways that it has the potential to be. I want you to feel mastery, to enjoy working with people because they are enthusiastically responding to you and rapidly doing what you need them to do. I want you to migrate that mastery to others, who will see you as a role model. I want you to become a highly valued individual, a trusted advisor and a well-respected resource. I want you to get exactly what you want.

If your appetite for success is whetted by this quick start guide and you want more examples, details, expert tips and techniques, you may purchase the full edition of *Speak Up! and Succeed: How to Get Everything You Want in Meetings, Presentations and Conversations*. For that and more, visit www.NanceSpeaks.com. I hope to see you at one of my speaking engagements, seminars or workshops, or have the opportunity to participate in one of your conferences, trainings or events.

If you want expert support for your marketing, sales and product portfolio programs and employee satisfaction and human resources programs, visit www.NAXpartners.com to see my firm's capabilities. I am the managing partner at NAX Partners, where we create the strategic, tactical and performance programs you need to reach your target markets, attract strategic partners, get access to investors and create the motivated, satisfied and loyal employees who will carry out your mission.

You may also contact me toll-free at: 1-888-GO NANCE.

No matter what road you take to success, even though it may be very different than mine, I'll look for you at the finish line!

Nance Rosen
Beverly Hills, California

CHAPTER ONE

Speak Up!

The right words delivered in the right way will change the course of your life. Every dream, goal or idea you have is simply sentences away from coming true.

If you only passively listen to what others are saying, you might *survive* in business, but to *thrive* at work, you must express yourself in a crisp, clear and compelling way.

Every great enterprise has a leader who uses words that drive others to take action exactly as that leader desires. These people prove that any amount of resistance from anyone can be overcome. Even the most negative situations you face can be transformed into perfect outcomes when you Speak Up in the right way at the right time.

- The foundation of success is knowing exactly what you want for yourself and from others.
- The fastest way to gain others' trust, agreement and cooperation is the Speak Up System. To make the maximum impact on your audience so they will listen and take action exactly as you desire, you use three acts: 1) your great opening; 2) your streamlined content; and 3) your great closing.

CHAPTER TWO

Listening Traps

Listening can be dangerous. Gurus who preach "active listening" techniques are leading you down the path to failure. When you let others endlessly express their thoughts and feelings, you're trapped like a caged lion. Instead, be an "assertive listener." Ask questions that lead to information you need about the individual or issue you are pursuing and that can help you diagnose problems or teach you valuable new skills. After that, Speak Up!

Conducting business with an open mind is dangerous. If you form your opinions, plans and goals in reaction to what others say and do, you'll never enjoy the success you truly deserve. Identify the most desirable outcome *before* each meeting, presentation and conversation. Then keep it in mind as you interact with others. You will be a natural leader since you know the direction to take. With an outcome mind—as opposed to an open mind—you get what you want rapidly and easily.

When you identify an ideal outcome for each relationship, you can focus on those people who have the most significant effect on your potential for success. You know how much time to invest and how many interactions you must link together in order to achieve your desired outcome.

- Avoid Listening Traps—allowing someone to talk on and on while you just listen. You are vulnerable anytime you don't have an outcome in mind.
- Success is a two-part equation: the actions you take on your own plus the interactions you have with others. Plan to optimize your performance in each part and follow your plan.

CHAPTER THREE

Showstoppers

Showstoppers are questions or statements that surprise others with your insight about a significant problem (misery) and its potential solution (remedy). They increase the respect and trust you get from others even when you aren't in charge or tapped to lead a meeting, presentation or conversation.

Typical misery triggers in any company include losing a major account (pain), facing the need for changing a system or policy (fear) or finding out that a goal has been reached by a competitor (unfulfilled desire).

Misery shines a harsh light on the gap between someone's real life and their ideal life. Most people yearn to bridge that gap to not only solve immediate problems but to get evidence that they are putting their values into action. There are five universal business values that drive people to take action: the desire for empowerment, security, vitality, creativity and individuality.

Your showstopper must sensitively address your audience's immediate misery and provide at least a small way to actualize one of those values. That combination is what makes your contribution so powerful and memorable.

A great showstopper is the pivotal question, which uses the "what if" approach to problem solving and connects your recommendation to a value. For example, you may see this pain in your organization: many employees suffer from information overload and fail to act on key initiatives. In a meeting to discuss productivity, a great pivotal question is: "Would it empower our managers and improve employee performance if everyone had one easy-to-read report?"

- A showstopper is a brief, powerful and memorable statement or question.
- An example of a showstopper is the pivotal question, which allows you to take center stage for a brief time, often changing the direction of the meeting, presentation or conversation.
- Over time, showstoppers earn you a reputation for being insightful, dedicated and trustworthy.

CHAPTER FOUR

The Backbone of Your Success

In the Speak Up System, we use the term "audience" to describe all of the people—one or more—with whom you speak in any meeting, presentation or conversation. In every interaction, your desired outcome is to move your audience closer to your point of view until you have exactly what you want.

In each of the following chapters, we go into greater detail about the Speak Up System. This chapter introduces you to the general framework and key concepts of the System.

The Transformation Channel

If your audience has any resistance to you or your desired outcome, you will need to successfully move them through five stages of transformation.

To get what you want, you must lead your audience through:

Stage One: Attention

You must get them focused on you.

Stage Two: Knowledge

You must provide a foundation of facts that bring them up to speed.

Stage Three: Preference

You must show them why your approach is better than alternatives.

Stage Four: Conviction

You must lead them to believe that unless they act now, they will risk losing out entirely.

Stage Five: Action

You must give them instructions and watch them comply.

The Three Acts of the Speak Up System

To subtly move your audience through the Transformation Channel, the Speak Up System uses three acts that make you appear well organized, crisp and confident. The following are the stages you must move them through during each act.

Act One: Your Great Opening (Attention)

Segment One: Introduce yourself (do this in new ways if they already know you)
Segment Two: Introduce your topic
Segment Three: Make promises

Act Two: Your Streamlined Content (Knowledge, Preference and Conviction)

Cull content from your Library of Success, which is where you store everything you need for each issue or topic that matters to you. The Library organizes your content into ten sections, each with a specific purpose.

Act Three: Your Great Closing (Action)

Segment One: Recall promises kept
Segment Two: Offer more value
Segment Three: Give instructions and get results

Four Dimensions of Decision-Making

To help you choose and deliver content that will have the maximum impact on your audience (and speed them through the Transformation Channel), there are four key areas to consider before you Speak Up.

Dimension 1: Player Profiles

You will face five different types of people in your audiences. You can customize your content to suit each of them.

Dimension 2: Interaction Style

Depending on the transformation you require, you may structure your interaction in a persuasive, team, training or briefing style.

Dimension 3: The Ideal Leadoff Component

From all of the content you intend to deliver, pick the tidbit your audience will find most significant and newsworthy but not too touchy.

Dimension 4: Use of Time and Tempo/Style

Divide your time this way: fifteen percent for your great opening, seventy percent for your streamlined content, and fifteen percent for your great closing. Vary your speed, pitch and volume as you move through your content.

CHAPTER FIVE

Start with Act One: Your Great Opening

Act one of the Speak Up System is your great opening. With your first words, you grab your audience's attention and make them feel lucky to hear from you. By the end of act one, you must have your audience's commitment to listen all the way through to your great closing. You do this by teasing them with a brief story, dramatic quotation or startling statistic to introduce yourself and your topic. Then, you connect their pain, fear or unfulfilled desire with your promise to give them the tools and solutions they need. You may need to amplify their misery so they are sorely in touch with how much they need to hear what you have to say.

Act one, your great opening, has three segments:

1. Introduce yourself: Inspire confidence and appear interesting. You must not only be capable of delivering important information, but you must also have an engaging way of presenting it.
2. Introduce your topic: Make your audience eager to pay attention by connecting your topic to their misery: a pain, fear or unfulfilled desire.
3. Make promises: Guarantee that by the end of the presentation your audience will have exactly what they need to solve a specific problem. If you are dealing with a complex issue that will take several interactions to remedy, plan on making incremental progress in each of the linked interactions.

CHAPTER SIX

Getting to Know You

The best way to introduce yourself to an audience is through a great story that describes an accomplishment or result you achieved in the face of significant odds. This is your heroic achievement story. Engage your audience and inspire confidence as you share the salient details of solving a problem to which they can relate.

How to present your heroic achievement story:

1. Tell the story in chronological order.
2. Set the scene: Describe the setting and what made the situation or conditions a problem for you or your company.
3. Add details about specific problems: What particular risks or consequences did you have to confront?
4. Explain how you resolved the problem. What solution did you invent, create or select? Describe the excellent result as well as how you achieved it as quickly as possible and at the smallest possible expense.
5. Introduce yourself: Tell the audience your name and job title or the focus of your work.
6. Highlight a key benefit or quality that makes you and your story universally appealing. Since heroic achievement stories are about specific events, what general achievement is at the heart of your story? Use that as the moral to ignite the belief that you are definitely worth their time.

CHAPTER SEVEN

Shock and Awe

When you are short on time or very familiar to your audience, introduce yourself with startling statistics that inspire their belief that you know something they don't. Alternatively, reveal something positive about your character and unique perspective by sharing a dramatic quotation that hints at how you will approach the concerns and problems of your audience.

Startling Statistics

- Use numbers or percentages to accurately and crisply provide a little-known fact that impacts your audience, whether they knew it or not.
- Metrics are universally understood and instantly inspire confidence.
- Compile a list of your own inspiring statistics, just like a professional athlete or stellar sports team would.

Dramatic Quotations

- Use a famous quotation to impress audiences with the depth of your intelligence and breadth of your interests.
- Create your own pithy quotation to surprise and impress your audience when you reveal that the author is you.
- Select a quote that represents skills or attitudes that matter to your audience, such as ingenuity, dedication or caring. This telegraphs how you will approach your audience's needs or problems.

CHAPTER EIGHT

The Big Tease

The best way to introduce your topic is to focus your audience on their misery (pain, fear or unfulfilled desire). Do it indirectly by telling a story or sharing a tidbit that amplifies their urgency to deal with the misery. Tease them with the hope that a happy ending is possible.

The following are five brief and interesting ways to introduce your topic.

Dramatic Story

This involves a victim whose problem was diagnosed and solved by the hero of the story—ideally you or your organization.

Startling Statistic

This method is useful when your audience believes a problem is only a minor annoyance or when players are afraid to admit they have a problem. Use your statistics to create concern or fear about unforeseen consequences or the unknown magnitude of the problem.

Nugget

This exclusive, time-sensitive or unusual fact can help create immediate interest in a new product or feature.

Surprising Example or Analogy

This approach is especially good for a training session or briefing, where your audience must master complex facts or technical information. The example or analogy creates a clear connection between something they already understand, perhaps from their daily routine or common sense, and what they are about to learn from you.

Success Story

Inspire players to use a new solution or approach that you recommend because it has already proven successful. This is especially effective when you feature a well-known authority, high-profile person or top-notch organization in your anecdote.

CHAPTER NINE

Promises, Promises

Making and keeping promises is not only the way we establish and build relationships, but it's also central to making a great presentation. In this third and last segment of your great opening, promise your audience that something real, useful and valuable will be theirs by the end of your time together. Be specific. Then, fulfill your promise in act two, your streamlined content.

In this segment, no matter what you have to say, find a way to characterize it as a remedy to some misery (pain, fear or unfulfilled desire) your audience is experiencing. For example, your proposed budget for a new information system can be morphed into a promise that by the end of your interaction they will be able to: 1) identify a key success factor to increasing revenue; 2) provide greater customer satisfaction; 3) solve a communication problem; or 4) increase the productivity of the workforce. Then, frame your promise this way: "By the end of our time together, I promise you will have an easy-to-implement solution to the problem you now face: getting the greatest productivity and profitability from all departments."

If time is too short for a big decision to be made in your favor, break the information and decision-making down into smaller increments that lead to that final decision. Just make sure to promise and deliver something valuable during each linked interaction along the way.

Tips on making promises:

- In the third and last segment of your great opening, use words like "promise," "guarantee" and "commitment."
- The most powerful promises offer a personal benefit to each player (e.g., private access codes to a technical help site) as well as significant benefits for their business, department or enterprise (e.g., bug-free technology).
- Tie your promise to the commitments and results you desire from them.
- Show them you are doing more than solving a problem: You are helping them put their values into action. At work, people are seeking empowerment, security, vitality, creativity and individuality. For example, "I promise that by the end of our time together today you'll have the tools to revitalize your organization's productivity and profitability. I guarantee you'll be empowered to make major changes in managing your company, simply by using your laptop or wireless device, no matter where you are in the world."

CHAPTER TEN

Key Questions for Crafting Promises

There are questions that are key when crafting promises in your great opening segment three. Your answers to these questions will help you decide what you want and when you should ask for specific commitments and actions.

Relationship Outcome

- What long-term result do you want from a particular audience?

Linked Interactions

- What incremental steps will lead to that outcome?
- What is the logical series of conversations, presentations and meetings you'll need, given your audience's understanding and inclination toward you and your goal?

Gateway Outcome

- What pivotal result will change the course of your relationship or accelerate it in the direction you desire?
- Will your breakthrough moment be the first sale, an approval to research a project or an interview with a hiring manager?

Proximate Outcome

- What results and commitments do you want from the particular interaction you are about to have?
- What can you get right now that will move you along the road to your relationship outcome?

Transformation

- How does your audience's mind-set need to change?
  - Are they negative and need to become positive?
  - Are they self-centered and need to become group goal oriented?
  - Are they deficient and need to become proficient?
  - Are they stuck and need to become proactive?

Content Components

- What specific bits of information, insights or references can you give your audience to move them through the five stages of transformation: 1) attention; 2) knowledge; 3) preference; 4) conviction; and 5) action?

CHAPTER ELEVEN

Act Two:
Deliver Streamlined Content

Via your great opening, you've plunged your audience into the Transformation Channel. You've gotten their *attention* (stage one). Now, from your streamlined content, they'll gain *knowledge* (stage two), develop a *preference* for your solution (stage three) and feel the *conviction* to act now or risk losing out (stage four). In act three, you'll provide instructions that satisfy their urgent need to take *action* (stage five). To use your time optimally, choose the content components that are most effective for the transformation you require:

- Persuasive interactions should include success stories; third-party standards and evaluations; and hands-on practice.
- Team interactions should include questions and answers; samples; and roadmaps and timelines.
- Training interactions should include assessments of your audience's abilities; step-by-step instructions; and a list of do's and don'ts.
- Briefing interactions should include a comparison of alternatives; forecasts; and recommendations.

In act two, your streamlined content must provide the information and experiences that create:

- Cognitive-Emotive Impact: both thinking and feeling responses from your audience.
- Sticky Decisions: lasting changes in your audience's mind-set.

CHAPTER TWELVE

Expressions that Leave Lasting Impressions

As you deliver content, make a lasting impression by involving more of your audiences' senses than hearing alone.

Whenever possible, use visuals, such as charts, slides and props, to illuminate your presentation. Increase your audience's involvement to accelerate their transformation. Role-play, view taped testimonials and share refreshments to fully engage your audience.

Tips for making memories:

- Use a prop to help describe a technical detail or concept.
- Have your audience help you perform an experiment, design a system or give input that you incorporate into your solution.
- Don't be afraid to get messy—just use a drop cloth that can catch the goop.

CHAPTER THIRTEEN

Your Library of Success

Create a personal library to store the content you need for your meetings, presentations and conversations. Begin by writing down all the topics you plan to address. Then, for each topic, jot down your content components, which are facts, stories, examples, samples and other materials that help support your point of view, proposals or plans. Appendix 1 has a list of components and shows you how to organize them under each section heading.

The sections of your Library of Success are named for their purpose:

1. Accountability
2. Comparisons
3. Credibility
4. Demonstrations
5. Downsides
6. Insights
7. Inspiration
8. Interactivity
9. Logic
10. Tips

- Your Library helps you quickly prepare yourself for any interaction.
- Memorize the most important content so you'll be ready to Speak Up at a moment's notice.
- If information is missing for one or more of the sections, don't worry. You can always add to your Library when you have time.

CHAPTER FOURTEEN

Decisions, Decisions

How do you decide which components will be most effective for each interaction and audience? Use the Four Dimensions of Decision-Making:

1. Player Profiles: What personality type do you face?

- Ducks: need success stories to follow.
- Peacocks: need big ideas and graphics.
- Woodpeckers: need technical details.
- Owls: need long-term forecasts.
- Chicken Littles: need total cost and use analysis.

2. Interaction Style: What resistance do you face?

Negative or Indifferent

- Use persuasive style
- Content components: success stories; endorsements; examples; invention or discovery stories; and total use and cost analysis.

Deficient or Naïve

- Use training style
- Content components: step-by-step instructions; demonstrations; hands-on practice; assessments; questions and answers; and role-play.

Self-Centered or Disconnected

- Use team style
- Content components: data with analysis; technical drawings; comparison of competition; communication facilitation; and roadmaps and timelines.

Stuck or Inactive

- Use briefing style
- Content components: comparison of alternatives; contrary data or conclusions; risk analysis; analogies; total cost and use analysis; and contracts.

3. Ideal Leadoff Component: What will lock in their interest?

- Lead off your content with a component that registers above simmering but doesn't ignite boiling reactions from your audience.

4. Time and Tempo/Style: Do you have five minutes or more?

- Use fifteen percent of your time for your great opening, seventy percent for your streamlined content and fifteen percent for your great closing.
- Vary the "music" of your language: your pace, pitch and volume. For example, technical content requires you to slow down, while success stories should be peppy.

CHAPTER FIFTEEN

Dimension 1: Player Profiles Birds of Different Feathers

Identify your players by their primary personality traits so you can tailor your content to their tastes. They will be engaged longer and lower their resistance when an interaction keeps their interest. To make this profiling easy to remember, players are classified as birds with similar characteristics: ducks, woodpeckers, peacocks, owls and "chicken littles."

Who is your audience and what appeals to them?

Ducks

- Followers who take time to jump in, shop around and get a lot of buy-in from others before proceeding.
- Effective content components: success stories; testimonials; and third-party standards.

Woodpeckers

- Constantly poke holes in others' assertions and are persistent and predictable.
- Effective content components: data with analysis; and technical drawings.

Peacocks

- Flashy and attention grabbing, incredibly impatient with details and quick to give approval or deny permission.
- Effective content components: graphics; samples; and props.

Owls

- Wise, principled and philosophical, learned in many disciplines and topics. Future oriented, they need a long time to make decisions.
- Effective content components: people profiles; roadmaps; and letters of agreement.

Chicken Littles

- Worriers and multi-taskers. They doubt that others grasp the big picture. With your content, help them gain confidence that you covered all of the bases.
- Effective content components: references; results and rewards lists; and contracts.

If you don't know your players, prepare your content for ducks, since most people like to do things that are already tried and true.

CHAPTER SIXTEEN

Dimension 2: Interaction Styles
Feather Your Nest

Depending upon your desired outcome and the resistance you anticipate, one of four interaction styles will deliver the transformation you need. The more resistant your audience is, the more linked interactions you will need. Often you'll need more than one interaction style to get everything you desire.

Before each meeting, presentation or conversation, consider your audience's mind-set. What transformation do you require for the actions and commitments you desire?

1. *Persuasive style* transforms an audience from negative to positive, or from bored or indifferent to enthusiastic. Include content from your inspiration and credibility sections.
2. *Team style* transforms an audience from disconnected to unified, or from self-centered to group goal oriented. Include content from your interactivity and accountability sections.
3. *Training style* transforms an audience from deficient to proficient, or from unsure to confident. Include content from your demonstrations and tips sections.
4. *Briefing style* transforms an audience from partially informed to updated, or from stuck or inactive to proactive. Include content from your comparisons and downsides sections.

- Don't let your job description determine the style you choose for your audience. For example, sales people don't sell all the time—sometimes they brief potential customers on the benefits of new products. Team leaders often train their teams on new skills before setting them to work on a task. Trainers may first persuade a group that training is crucial. Executives who resist change may first need to be persuaded before you can brief them on the alternatives.

CHAPTER SEVENTEEN

Dimension 3: Your Ideal Leadoff Component Hot Topics

What issue or approach will lock in your audience's interest? You may need to re-characterize your topic so players find it compelling and so you kick off act two—your streamlined content—with a bang.

Evaluate your content and select the ideal leadoff component by judging your audience's reactivity to these three aspects:

1. Sensitivity: Are players willing to talk about the topic or listen to a presentation? If there's been a failure or misstep, they may be too sensitive to your addressing the issue straight-on. Choose a component from your inspiration section and avoid one from accountability.
2. Significance: Are players bored by the topic, or is it a priority in their lives? If they don't seem motivated, choose a component from downsides or accountability so your topic becomes an urgent issue.
3. Freshness: Are players tired of reviewing the topic? Is it ancient history or a bad memory? If so, craft a "breaking-news flash" using content from your comparisons or insights sections.

CHAPTER EIGHTEEN

Dimension 4: Time and Tempo/Style Keep It Humming

Anytime you have five minutes or more, you can Speak Up and Succeed. However, the amount of time you have influences the amount of transformation you can ignite in your audience. You may need to link several interactions in order to arrive at your relationship outcome, but with a proximate outcome for each link, you ensure steady progress toward your long-term goal.

The following are some tips for ensuring each of your interactions is as productive as it can be:

- Keep your presentation clear and compelling, cutting out non-essential components. This lean approach proves to your audience that you only deliver the best, regardless of the time available. That's part of what creates your reputation as a trusted advisor.
- Vary your pace, pitch and volume as you go through your content. Consider what tempo each component requires for maximum absorption by your audience. For example, be lively for inspiration components, moderately slow for comparisons and brisk for tips. This change-up amplifies the meaning of your content and improves your audience's retention and involvement.
- Deliver your ideal leadoff component using a snappy and energetic speed.
- Variety is more satisfying than one constant rhythm as you go through content.
- Create pauses during your presentation so your audience can use that time to process what you've delivered.

CHAPTER NINETEEN

Finish with Act Three: Your Great Closing

Just like a great movie, a great presentation builds to a satisfying ending. Keep your audience engaged to the last minute so that they will eagerly comply when you give instructions to take action and will keep their commitments when they leave you.

Act three, your great closing, has three segments:

1. Recall promises kept: Remind your audience about the opening promises you made and highlight how you fulfilled those promises throughout the interaction.
2. Offer more value: Provide unexpected handouts, expert advice and special offers so your audience receives much more than they anticipated.
3. Give instructions and get results: Tell your audience what to do now that they have the knowledge, preference and conviction needed to take action. Make it easy for them to follow through. Have all the documents, sign-up sheets and assignments typed up and photocopied, as well as pens, staplers and giveaways available right there.

CHAPTER TWENTY

Fresh Memories

To launch your great closing, remind your audience about the promises you made during your opening and how your presentation fulfilled those promises. Keep it short and to the point.

This first segment of your great closing is meant to tip the relationship scale, which is the balance between what you are offering in exchange for what your audience is offering: their time and attention. Your goal is to load on what you delivered and underscore what your audience has or can now do as a result of your interaction.

You want to make two things clear. First, you want your audience to feel that you are a trusted advisor who delivers as promised. Second, you want them to believe that their values have been put into action. Ideally, your audience has been empowered with material that increases their entity's vitality and security. Hopefully, they have gained some creative approaches and new ways to express their individual talent or ability, which should increase the recognition they receive from their organization, department or colleagues.

- Repeat the promises you made in your great opening's segment three. For example, say, "As you recall when we first began, I promised . . ."
- Highlight, don't summarize, your entire presentation. Just identify the content components that fulfilled your promises. For example, you could say, "The success stories proved . . ."
- Your goal is to amplify players' recollections of your contribution. That primes them to reciprocate.

CHAPTER TWENTY-ONE

Take That!

Now is the time to surprise your audience with added value. Offer an extra gift that is connected to the action you're driving them toward. For example, if you want them to trial your new software, offer each person a gift card that has an access code to your Web site. The card is activated when the user completes a trial of your software.

With this "sweetener" coming on top of everything else you provided, your audience's expectations have been exceeded. By tipping the relationship scale so much in their favor, you have invoked the rule of reciprocity, which is the instinctive response to return a favor. Your audience is going to balance the scale by giving you what you want. Thus, you have prepared them to follow your instructions when you get to the last segment of your great closing.

- Make it clear that you are offering an extra gift.
- Identify yourself as the gift giver.
- Imply that there are conditions to be met for receiving the gift. The conditions will be giving you what you want—what you planned as the outcome—for this interaction.
- Tell them what the extra gift is.
- Gifts can be:
  - Tangible: Software, gift certificates, commemorative pins and the like.
  - Intangible: The opportunity to win at a game, contest or drawing.
  - Connections and access: Free additional training, networking, personal support, access to proprietary information and similar perks.

CHAPTER TWENTY-TWO

Get What's Coming to You

Your audience is now ready to buy. Once you give instructions, stop talking so that everyone can follow them. Don't do or say anything to distract them from immediately taking action. You don't want them to hesitate because they feel you might have something more to share. Any hesitation you cause in this final segment will delay or possibly even completely deny you the outcome you've been driving toward.

The third segment of your great closing is simply to give instructions and get results.

- Make your instructions simple and clear so that your players behave the way you want them to behave.
- To increase compliance, use the word "because" followed by a brief reason to further guide them. For example, you could say, "Go to the back of the room to sign up for your installation." However, you will get a stronger response if you say, "Go to the back of the room to sign up for your installation *because* the list we take home today will get priority treatment."
- Repeat your instructions twice to fix your plan in the minds of your audience.
- Stop talking and allow time for everyone to complete the task you set for them.
- Finish your great closing with an enthusiastic confirmation like "Great!" or "Well done!"
- Be prepared with pens, business cards, a computer connected to the Internet or whatever else is required to assist your audience in taking action with ease.
- Briefly answer last-minute questions from individuals and say your good-byes.

Congratulations! You are now ready to become a Speak Up Star. Put the system to work and you can count on getting everything you want in meetings, presentations and conversations.

APPENDICES

APPENDIX 1

Library of Success

Accountability

Budgets BD
Contracts CN
Forecasts FO
Letters of Agreement LA
Proposals PA
Roadmaps and Timelines RT
Specifications SP
Total Cost of Purchase and Use Analysis TC

Comparisons

Comparison of Alternative Courses of Action CA
Comparison of Competition CC

Credibility

People Profiles PF
References RE
Testimonials and Endorsements TE
Third-Party Standards and Evaluations TH

Demonstrations

Features, Functions and Benefits FB
Product Demonstrations PR
Proprietary Processes or Parts PP
Samples SA

Downsides

Contrary Data or Conclusions CD
Plan Bs PB
Risk Analysis RA

Insights

Analogies AN
Examples EX
Graphics, Photos, Animation and Artwork GA
Props PS
Recommendations RC
Resources RS
Video and Audio VA

Inspiration

Invention or Discovery Stories ID
Motivating Misery Triggers MM
Rewards and Results Stories and Lists RR
Success Stories, Applications and Case Histories SS

Interactivity

Assessments AS
Audience Experiences AE
Communication Facilitation CF
Hands-On Practice HO
Premium PM
Questions and Answers QA
Questionnaires QS
Role-Play RP

Logic

Blueprints or Technical Drawings BT
Data with Analysis DD
Facts and Figures FF
Technical Data TD

Tips

Lists of Do's and Don'ts LD
Step-by-Step Instructions ST
Techniques, Advanced TN
Tips, Secrets and Hints TS

APPENDIX 2.1

Persuasive-Style Interaction

Speak Up Star

Bank executive Josh Kitulak makes a persuasive-style presentation to homeowners and small-business owners.

Relationship Outcome: Sales of loans and other financial products
Gateway Outcome: Get individuals to apply for loans

Dimensions of Decision-Making

Audience: Mainly ducks, some other profiles
Mind-Set Transformation: Negative to positive, indifferent to enthusiastic
Interaction Style: Persuasive
Ideal Leadoff Component: Rewards and Results Stories and Lists (RR)
Time: 1 hour
Tempo/Style: Staccato to Vivace

Opening Segment One: Allegro

"The best investment on earth is earth," or so said Louis Glickman, a famous real-estate investor.[1] Maybe that is your belief and you want to own real estate or own more real estate. Or, maybe you believe that the best investment is one you make in yourself or your family members, such as getting an education. Perhaps you want to pursue a dream to open or enlarge your own business.

Opening Segment Two: Spirito

What if you had just one chance—the chance of your lifetime—to earn and put away all the money you would ever need to feel secure, to support yourself and your family, to live the life of your dreams? A farmer in Wichita Falls, Kansas, lost that chance when he went bankrupt because his crop failed and he could not pay the mortgage on his property. That man was my neighbor, someone who was good, and decent and almost like a father to me. He became my inspiration for building a bank that was more than a debt collector.

At First Farm and Commerce Bank, we know that today might be your one chance of a lifetime to get the right financing from a lender. Do you want to see how you can achieve your goals? Do you want to ensure that you don't lose your security and your hope for a wonderful life?

Opening Segment Three: Staccato

That's why I'm here today, and I hope that's why you're here as well. I want you to see that if your dreams and goals involve making an investment, you are going to have a friend and trusted advisor in me and the other professionals at First Farm and Commerce. I guarantee that today you are going to get the facts about how to borrow the funds you need without fearing that you can't afford such an investment in your future. Do you think your dreams are worth investing in?

Streamlined Content

Fully present the italicized components and highlight + hand out the remaining ones.

Rewards and Results Stories and Lists (RR): Vivace
Success Stories, Applications and Case Histories (SS): Spirito
People Profiles (PF): Allegro
Testimonials and Endorsements (TE): Presto
Communication Facilitation (CF): Allegro
Questions and Answers (QA): Allegro
Facts and Figures (FF): Andante
Lists of Do's and Don'ts (LD): Allegro
Step-by-Step Instructions (ST): Staccato
Assessments (AS)
Budgets (BD)
Total Cost of Purchase and Use Analysis (TC)

Closing Segment Three: Vivace

Do you feel that if you'd known this sooner, you'd be further along toward your goals and truly enjoying a wonderful life? I told you that today you were going to get the facts you needed and lose the fear that you couldn't afford your dreams.

Closing Segment Two: Spirito

I'd like to make this simple and easy for you so that you can get on to living your dreams as quickly as possible. If you start the loan application today, you will receive a three-month grace period before any payment is due. That's three months to use the funds, without any payment due, if you are approved.

Closing Segment Three: Andante

Just go ahead and take the forms. Before you leave, complete the top sheet and turn it in to me. That way you're going to get that three-month grace period and get ready to live your dream. I'll be here to help answer any questions you have about the form.

[1] "The best investment on earth is earth," Louis Glickman, real estate investor, in *New York Post*, 3 September 1957.

APPENDIX 2.2

Persuasive-Style Interaction

Speak Up Star

Engineer Todd Lilaw persuades IT tradeshow visitors to consider an updated software package.

Relationship Outcome: Use demonstration at company booth to launch sales effort

Proximate Outcome: (Link 1 on relationship map) Assembled visitors move on to sales rep Tony Michaels to set appointments

Dimensions of Decision-Making

Audience: Ducks, woodpeckers

Mind-Set Transformation: Negative to positive, indifferent to enthusiastic

Interaction Style: Persuasive

Ideal Leadoff Component: Product Demonstrations (PR)

Time: 20 minutes

Tempo/Style: Andante to Vivace

Opening Segment One: Allegro

To sharpen your company's edge over competition, you may choose to follow author Theodore Roszak's exclamation about technology: "What can be done, must be done."

Opening Segment Two: Presto

If your patches and workarounds are failing to revitalize your system, you can now do what must be done.

Opening Segment Three: Spirito

By the end of our time together today, I guarantee you will have a new tool—one that lets you identify the root cause of your worst problem: system failure. Plus, you will have the power to solve that problem and generate production that exceeds your company's current goals.

Streamlined Content

Fully present all components.

Product Demonstrations (PR): Allegro

Rewards and Results Stories and Lists (RR): Spirito

Hands-On Practice (HO): Allegro

Closing Segment One: Allegro

When we first came together today, I guaranteed you would have a new tool—one that lets you identify the root cause of your system failure. In fact, you mastered that skill today when you took time for hands-on practice with the software diagnostic program. When you take the demo back to your office, you can run it on your own system. With those results, you will pinpoint the leaks and use the prompts to model different solutions. Once that demo is in your hands, you will have the power to generate productivity that exceeds your current goals.

Closing Segment Two: Spirito

I'd like to offer you a package to take back to your office. In it, you'll find our software demonstration plus a gift certificate that you may redeem at several retailers or on the Web. It's our gesture of appreciation for your interest. Would you like to have those packages now?

Closing Segment Three: Spirito

Let's do that! Please proceed to the pod where you see all the green gift bags. You may pick up your package and gift certificate there.

APPENDIX 3.1

Training-Style Interaction

Speak Up Star

Department head Denise Buss trains customer service representatives on client service skills.

Relationship Outcome: Increase customer retention
Proximate Outcome: Learners exhibit negotiation skills and stress management

Dimensions of Decision-Making

Audience: Ducks, woodpeckers, chicken littles
Mind-Set Transformation: Unsure to confident
Interaction Style: Training
Ideal Leadoff Component: Motivating Misery Triggers (MM)
Time: 2 hours
Tempo/Style: Andante to Allegro

Opening Segment One: Spirito

The day began with a text message from manufacturing. My BlackBerry read: "We will not make the delivery as you promised to your largest customer." After a quick call, I turned off the highway that led to our office and instead drove directly to the customer. When I arrived, their management team had gotten my call and was waiting in the conference room. The first question I asked was: "How bad do you want it?" They laughed, because not everyone quotes a Don Henley song instead of trembling in their boots when they can't deliver what they promised. With that, the customer gave us three more days. We made that delivery—and the revenue. I'm Denise Buss, from the first graduating class of our Excellence Academy and I'm darn proud of that training.

Opening Segment Two: Presto

In our sector, it's as easy to retain a customer as it is to lose one. With odds like that, you may be the tipping point: the difference between the company being a stable and secure employer or not. You're going to find out two amazing truths today: The customer is one of the most important assets of this company, and so are you.

Opening Segment Three: Allegro

We want both you and the customer to thrive. That's why we're taking this time today to give you two tools that you cannot live without in this job. During the first half of our training, you are going to learn how to communicate with customers so that they feel assured that their interests are being taken care of by you and everyone else here at the company. During the second half of our training, you are going to learn how to reduce your stress—even prevent it—so that you can come in every day and look forward to your key role in our success. These are easy to master techniques, I promise.

Streamlined Content

Fully present italicized components and highlight + hand out the remaining ones.

Success Stories, Applications and Case Histories (SS): Spirito
Audience Experiences (AE): Andante
Hands-On Practice (HO): Allegro
Examples (EX): Staccato
Lists of Do's and Don'ts (LD)
Step-by-Step Instructions (ST)
Tips, Secrets and Hints (TS): Spirito
Techniques, Advanced (TN): Allegro

Closing Segment One: Staccato

I hope you feel that I kept my promise and that you have mastered the basic techniques of customer relations and stress management today. You saw the simple principles used in each of the case histories. As you experienced in the practice sessions, the details change but the issues are the same. And now, you have some advanced techniques to manage customers' complaints while keeping your own stress level down.

Closing Segment Two: Spirito

As we discussed, part of managing stress is healthy eating. I have an opportunity for six people in this room to win a free lunch at the sandwich restaurant in our office park. Does a free lunch sound good right now? And, remember to make it a healthy sandwich or salad.

Closing Segment Three: Andante

Simply complete the evaluation form in your packet. It will take three minutes. When you're done, fold your form in half, from top to bottom. Then fold it in half again, this time from the left side to the right side. Put your name on the outside of the form. You'll have a small rectangle just like this sample. When everyone has dropped a form into the bowl, I'll close my eyes and pick six forms out of it. Those lucky six win a free lunch. Let me entice you by waving these coupons. Now ready, set, evaluate!

APPENDIX 3.2

Training-Style Interaction

Speak Up Star

IT database manager Gary Singleton trains sales representatives on computer-assisted prospecting.

Relationship Outcome: Increase prospects in pipeline and telesales productivity
Proximate Outcome: Learners role-play using fundamentals of good communications

Dimensions of Decision-Making

Audience: Ducks, woodpeckers, peacocks
Mind-Set Transformation: Deficient to proficient
Interaction Style: Training
Ideal Leadoff Component: Success Stories, Applications and Case Histories (SS)
Time: 2 hours
Tempo/Style: Andante to Allegro

Opening Segment One: Allegro

Pablo Picasso said, "Computers are useless. They only give you answers."

Opening Segment Two: Spirito

Today, you are going to have the answer the most difficult question you face in sales: whom should I call? Who is the prospect most likely to lead to a sale?

Opening Segment Three: Staccato

Today you'll tap in to the database and discover a fast and easy way to increase and accelerate your revenue production. I promise that by the time we conclude today, you'll have a list of customers in your territory who are ready to purchase upgrades and who will welcome your call. I also guarantee you'll locate at least three strong prospects with a link to your current accounts—they're in sister companies. You'll become a master at generating the most profitable leads and be able to meet and exceed your quota.

Streamlined Content

Fully present italicized components and highlight + hand out the remaining ones.

Success Stories, Applications and Case Histories (SS): Vivace
Features, Functions and Benefits (FB): Allegro
Product Demonstrations (PR): Andante

Communication Facilitation (CF): Allegro
Questions and Answers (QA): Allegro
Hands-On Practice (HO): Andante
Lists of Do's and Don'ts (LD): Presto
Step-by-Step Instructions (ST): Staccato
Tips, Secrets and Hints (TS): Allegro
Techniques, Advanced (TN)
Specifications (SP)

Closing Segment One: Spirito

When we began this training, I promised a fast and easy way to increase and accelerate your revenue production. You got that as soon as you saw the system demonstration. I also promised that you would have a list of customers who would welcome your call because they are ready to purchase upgrades. By using your own territory's data in the hands-on practice, you got a list that you can start calling this very afternoon. I also guaranteed three strong prospects just from using the links to your current accounts. By using the step-by-step instructions, that's what you netted. Finally, I gave you my word that you will become a master at generating leads that result in your meeting and exceeding quota. With the advanced techniques supplied in your handout, you are ready to do just that.

Closing Segment Two: Presto

I've been empowered to offer an incentive for you to get on the phones right away and connect with these leads. You'll receive a two-percent increase over your usual commission on all leads that you convert during the next eight weeks.

Closing Segment Three: Andante

So, get cracking, and not just on the leads you found today, but also be sure to continue to use the system to generate as many other leads as you can. All the leads from your computer-based searches that you convert during the next eight weeks will net you an additional two-percent commission.

Please take my card so that if you run into any problems with the system, I'll be able to walk you through the process. In advance, let me congratulate you on whatever you're going to buy with that additional commission!

APPENDIX 4.1

Team-Style Interaction

Speak Up Star

Director of international operations Dave Meredith facilitates a team meeting with scientists and technicians.

Relationship Outcome: Gain commitment to rigorous work schedule and deadlines
Proximate Outcome: New product roadmap, working teams formed

Dimensions of Decision-Making

Audience: Primarily woodpeckers, some owls
Mind-Set Transformation: Disconnected to unified, self-centered to group goal oriented
Interaction Style: Team
Ideal Leadoff Component: Invention or Discovery Stories (ID)
Time: 3 days
Tempo/Style: Andante to Allegro

Opening Segment One: Allegro

"I would do anything to live a normal life for just one day." That's what I heard from a young girl entering high school with a body covered with eczema. Her arms and legs were scaly and raw. She could never wear anything but long-sleeved shirts and pants, covering not only her medical condition, but her shame at looking so different. Hello, I'm Dave Meredith, and I am glad you have come here to invest in that young lady's future as well as your own.

Opening Segment Two: Staccato

I don't know if you've ever seen a person injured in a chemical spill, but I can tell you that chemical burns are among the ugliest wounds a person can suffer. Until the government imposed safety protocols, workers were often blinded, scalded or disfigured because their workplaces had no emergency medical aid on the premises. When a family member was seriously injured in an acid spill on a metal processing production line, a Keck scientist took it upon himself to experiment with growing artificial skin cells. From that first personal mission, Keck has continued its dedication to developing leading-edge cures in dermatology. If you care about people—young and old—suffering with a skin disease, disorder or condition, your life may be about to change.

Opening Segment Three: Andante

You have been selected to be a part of a fast-track team here at Keck. You'll be given more freedom and more resources than other scientific staff. During our meeting today, I am going to reveal where our most significant research is leading and ask you to help shape it. Over the next three days, you are going to produce a roadmap of the disease states that you feel deserve our top priority. You will get to know each other very well, and at the end of our meeting will identify potential partners for your lab teams. The Keck Elite Research Conclave is now in session.

Streamlined Content

Fully present all components.

Invention or Discovery Stories (ID)
Third-Party Standards and Evaluations (TH)
Assessments (AS)
Communication Facilitation (CF)
Questionnaires (QS)
Proprietary Processes or Parts (PP)
Data with Analysis (DD)
Technical Data (TD)
Recommendations (RC)
Techniques, Advanced (TN)
Comparison of Alternative Courses of Action (CA)
Comparison of Competition (CC)
Contrary Data or Conclusions (CD)
Risk Analysis (RA)
Roadmaps and Timelines (RT)

Closing Segment One: Allegro

As I promised you when we began our conclave, you have seen the most significant research findings to date, which include our own proprietary processes, data and analysis and our competitors' activity. You have begun the process of shaping our future by contributing your own conclusions based on your instincts, experience, education and purpose. Together, we have filled out an aggressive roadmap, which will form the future of this company, your professional lives and the hope of our patients. I promised that you would also identify potential partners for your lab teams, which means aligning with those scientists and technicians who have interests similar to yours.

Closing Segment Two: Spirito

Our planning team will take the results of this meeting and advise you of the next step via e-mail. Now, I would like to offer you an expression of our confidence in you and our gratitude for your outstanding work this week, as well as for taking this time away from your family and friends. You and a guest are invited to our annual corporate meeting in Hawaii this February. You will be asked to attend a few meetings, but in large part we would like you enjoy the vacation and mix and mingle with the other members of this elite team. This will help you form relationships that will lead to selecting your lab teams.

Closing Segment Three: Presto

As you leave today, please pick up your packets from the logistics staff over there, and expect more details to come via e-mail. Next time we are together, surf's up!

APPENDIX 4.2

Team-Style Interaction

Speak Up Star

Project team captain Kevin Abramson facilitates a team meeting with multi-department staff who are late on a project.

Relationship Outcome: Deliver project on more realistic schedule, improve communication between departments and add resources as needed

Proximate Outcome: Revise product roadmap and assure commitment to delivery

Dimensions of Decision-Making

Audience: Ducks and woodpeckers

Mind-Set Transformation: Self-centered to group goal oriented

Interaction Style: Team

Ideal Leadoff Component: Invention or Discovery Stories (ID)

Time: 5 hours

Tempo/Style: Andante to Allegro

Opening Segment One: Spirito

George Washington wrote, "It is better to offer no excuse than a bad one." I am here to encourage you to get beyond what has gone wrong on this project. Let's use this time to learn what's needed to help you succeed.

Opening Segment Two: Staccato

You may not know that the founder of our company was an engineer with no business training when he was making our first product in his basement and his wife was doing the books in the kitchen. He took a lot of wrong turns along the way, but he never felt he failed, because he saw every so-called failure lead to success.

Opening Segment Three: Presto

I promise this meeting will pay off by giving you exactly what you desire from this project. We will reframe the work plan so it accurately reflects the time and support you need. You'll have the opportunity to talk about the obstacles facing you, and we'll identify the resources or exchange information to overcome those obstacles. Before we leave, you'll approve a roadmap that guarantees you get what you need with minimum stress and maximum speed.

Streamlined Content

Fully present italicized components and highlight + hand out the remaining ones.

Invention or Discovery Stories (ID): Allegro
Third-Party Standards and Evaluations (TH): Staccato
Specifications (SP): Andante
Audience Experiences (AE): Spirito
Communication Facilitation (CF): Andante
Questions and Answers (QA): Andante
Facts and Figures (FF)
Analogies (AN): Presto
Technical Data (TD)
Recommendations (RC): Allegro
Plan Bs (PB): Andante
Roadmaps and Timelines (RT): Andante
Assessments (AS): Spirito

Closing Segment One: Allegro

This morning, I kicked off the meeting with three promises. First promise: you would get exactly what you desire from this project. From our rewards and results session, it's crystal clear that this project is highly desirable and is worth moving to the top of our list at full-speed ahead. Second promise: A forum to identify the obstacles facing you, and the resources and information you need to overcome those obstacles. The individual assessments and questionnaires revealed those. Third promise: a roadmap that not only sets out your deliverables but also schedules the time and materials you need at each juncture of the project. Thanks to a great communication facilitation by our project manager, here's our newly completed roadmap that minimizes stress and maximizes speed.

Closing Segment Two: Presto

To commemorate our new vision, I'd like to give each of you a specially designed polo-style shirt. You can see that each one is embroidered with your name and the motto management has for this team: "Less Haste, More Speed." We hope that reminds you that we want you to work at maximum efficiency, but not burn out your ability to do the great work of which you are capable.

Closing Segment Three: Andante

You have received an evaluation form, which you must complete before you leave. You'll see that it asks questions about the results from today's meeting. This will assure us that you are returning to the project with no loose ends or unaddressed concerns. When you've completed the form, please come up and receive your team shirt.

APPENDIX 5.1

Briefing-Style Interaction

Speak Up Star

Property manager Jim Gabriel briefs business visitors at his corporate park in Kentucky.

Relationship Outcome: Show advantage of setting up corporate offices in office park
Proximate Outcome: Get visitors to attend evening reception; get favorable evaluation

Dimensions of Decision-Making

Audience: Mainly ducks but group includes all five profiles
Mind-Set Transformation: Partially informed to updated
Interaction Style: Briefing
Ideal Leadoff Component: Rewards and Results Stories and Lists (RR)
Time: 1 hour
Tempo/Style: Andante to Vivace

Opening Segment One: Vivace

Kentucky is the home of Churchill Downs, which is where the world comes to watch the most exciting two minutes in sports: the famous Kentucky Derby.

Opening Segment Two: Andante

In December 2004, the Kentucky Equine Education Project formally announced what many citizens of our state already know from their pay stubs: The Kentucky Derby is a $127 million payday for the state of Kentucky's economy.

Racetracks and horse farms employ over 140,000 people. That number does not take into account other related companies and jobs—insurance, hospitality, media and more—that serve those people. Every sector of business is represented here. Why have all these companies flocked to the Bluegrass State? What do they know that you should know?

Opening Segment Three: Spirito

Today, I promise you'll find out why companies are happy to be here. You'll receive a treasure trove of information and a very special invitation.

Streamlined Content

Fully present italicized components and highlight + hand out the remaining ones.

Rewards and Results Stories and Lists (RR): Vivace
Success Stories, Applications and Case Histories (SS): Spirito

People Profiles (PF): Staccato
Testimonials and Endorsements (TE)
Audience Experiences (AE): Allegro
Communication Facilitation (CF): Presto
Questions and Answers (QA): Presto
Tips, Secrets and Hints (TS): Vivace
Total Cost of Purchase and Use Analysis (TC): Andante
Letters of Agreement (LA)
Contracts (CN)

Closing Segment One: Staccato

You've heard the success stories of so many companies that are doing well in our corporate park. You've met our people through their profiles and asked some excellent questions. I hope you enjoyed the virtual tour of the development we're building now.

Closing Segment Two: Spirito

As I promised, I'd like to extend a special invitation to you that we hope you'll find hard to turn down. You're invited to be our guest at the Kentucky Horse Park, where you'll meet the world's most esteemed champions, including Horses of the Year Cigar and John Henry, among others. Would you like that?

Closing Segment Three: Andante

Great! You'll find tickets in each of the packets, which also contain more information on our property and an evaluation of your tour today. I appreciate your completing the evaluation so my company has your valuable feedback on this presentation.

APPENDIX 5.2

Briefing-Style Interaction

Speak Up Star

Design chief Jennie Berman briefs her CEO on an acquisition candidate.

Relationship Outcome: Radically depart from the company's technology platform

Proximate Outcome: CEO gives his permission for Jennie to initiate negotiations with a small design firm that has a patent on leading-edge technology

Dimensions of Decision-Making

Audience: CEO, an owl
Mind-Set Transformation: Inactive to proactive
Interaction Style: Briefing
Ideal Leadoff Component: Forecasts (FO)
Time: 40 minutes
Tempo/Style: Andante to Allegro

Opening Segment One: Andante

Have you read this quote from Thoreau? "What recommends commerce to me is its enterprise and bravery."

Opening Segment Two: Andante

In the face of our pilot program failure, we are in danger of being eclipsed by a small competitor that doesn't have our overhead but that wants our customers.

Opening Segment Three: Spirito

By the end of this briefing, I guarantee you'll have a clear picture of our company's market position and a reliable forecast of our position for the next five years. Using that information, you'll be able to make decisions that help fulfill our company's goals for growth and stability.

Streamlined Content

Fully present italicized components and highlight + hand out the remaining ones.

Roadmaps and Timelines (RT)
Data with Analysis, expert (DD): Presto
Assessments by executive team (AS): Allegro
Forecasts (FO): Andante

Third-Party Standards and Evaluations (TH)
Proprietary Processes or Parts (PP)
Contrary Data or Conclusions (CD)
Comparison of Alternative Courses of Action (CA)

Closing Segment One: Presto

When we commenced today's briefing, I promised that you would have a clear picture of our company's market position and have a reliable forecast of our position through the upcoming five years. Using the expert's analysis and the executive team's assessments, you saw for yourself how the technology roadmap and timeline play out. We pinpointed exactly where we are and examined the forecast that shows where we are headed.

Closing Segment Two: Andante

I'd like to offer a traditional route to pursuing more growth and revenue: discreetly looking at potential acquisition candidates. I have the profile on a very promising one here, with solid technology and owners who can invent but really need our infrastructure and management. Would you like to see it?

Closing Segment Three: Vivace

Great. The next step is to pick up the phone and pay a visit to their offices. Let's do that while we're together now. Let's pick up the phone and arrange a visit with them.

GLOSSARY

3P Soup: Each player's profile includes a mix of personality, preferences and peccadilloes. (*See also* peccadilloes, personality and preferences.)

Actions: What you want your audience to do by the end of your interaction. Also, those tasks you do on your own, including things like writing, creating spreadsheets, operating machinery, researching information or reading documents. Actions are one-half of your personal equation of success.

Active Listening: An approach to communication that attempts to give others the impression that you understand and appreciate their points of view. You nod, take notes and parrot back key points. Unfortunately, you risk affirming their opinions and bolstering their beliefs. Therefore, you may be undermining your own desired course of action.

Allegro: Lively; a brisk walking speed. Good for inspiration and credibility. (*See also* model speak up orchestration.)

Andante: Moderately slow; a normal walking speed. Best when sharing comparisons, downsides and contracts. (*See also* model speak up orchestration.)

Assertive Listening: Asking questions to get the information you need so you can guide the discussion where you want it to go.

Audience: Everyone in your meetings, presentations or conversations, whether it's 1 or 1,000 people.

Backbone of Success: The Speak Up System, including the three acts you use to organize an interaction. Act one: your great opening; act two: your streamlined content; act three: your great closing. These acts organize your contribution so you easily slip your audience into the Transformation Channel and rapidly move them through it. Thus, you change their mind-sets from being resistant to compliant, and you get what you want. (*See also* Transformation Channel.)

Brain Clumps: Thoughts, feelings, beliefs and images assembled from education and experiences. By relating your topic to one of these brain clumps, you grab players' attention and anchor their commitment to stay with you through your great closing.

Briefing-Style Meeting: Changes your audience's mind-set from partially informed to updated and from stuck or inactive to proactive.

Chicken Littles: Worriers and multi-taskers who doubt that others grasp the big picture or can handle the details. (*See also* player profiles and players.)

Cognitive-Emotive Impact: The middle three stages of the Transformation Channel, where your content targets your audience's minds and hearts: *knowledge*, *preference* and *conviction*. (*See also* Transformation Channel.)

Compatibility: To be in line with a player's current thinking, culture or customs. (*See also* why-to-buys.)

Connections and Access: Networking a player to an individual or organization, or giving your audience entry into an exclusive part of a Web site.

Content Components: Specific bits of information, insights or references you give your audience to move them through a change in mind-set. Components are organized by their purpose into ten sections: inspiration, credibility, interactivity, demonstrations, logic, tips, comparisons, insights, downsides and accountability.

Creativity: Taking innovative and unusual approaches to problems or obstacles. (*See also* universal business values.)

Dangerous Questions: Propositions that are seen as challenges to authority or the status quo. These questions can provoke an argument, dismissal or dissent. Change dangerous questions into pivotal questions by inserting a value and asking what if? (*See also* pivotal questions.)

Dramatic Quotations: Famous quotes or ones you've created to reveal something about your character or perspective and that hint at how you will approach the concerns and problems of your audience.

Ducks: These are followers. They take time to jump in and shop around and get a lot of buy-in from others before proceeding. (*See also* player profiles and players.)

Easy Trial: A low-risk way to see if a product would work. (*See also* why-to-buys.)

Empowerment: The feeling of mastery, self-confidence and high self-esteem. (*See also* universal business values.)

Extra Gift: The sweetener, or unexpected added value, that you offer your audience to ignite their taking action as you desire. (*See also* intangible gifts and tangible gifts.)

Fear: The state of mind when a person or organization becomes acutely aware of a looming consequence, especially an imminent one that's likely to result in loss, misfortune or other pain. (*See also* Misery Triggers.)

Four Dimensions of Decision-Making: How to select the perfect mix of content components to accelerate results from any audience on any topic. The Four Dimensions are: 1) player profiles; 2) interaction style; 3) ideal leadoff component; and 4) time and tempo/style. (*See also* interaction style, player profiles, ideal leadoff component and time and tempo/style.)

Gateway Outcome: A major breakthrough that you plan to achieve during one of a series of linked interactions. This may be the first sale, even if it's small, or the first time you meet all the decision-makers and users.

Gateway Outcome Story: A story about another situation that focuses on a result that you see as a breakthrough for you with this audience.

Great Closing: The last part of your presentation (act three of the Speak Up System), when you get your audience to take the action you desire. In segment one, you reiterate the promises you made in your great opening and show how you fulfilled them with your content. In segment two, you add a sweetener, something they did not expect but definitely want. In segment three, you leverage that sweetener and give instructions so your audience knows exactly how to take action and give you the commitments you desire.

Great Opening: The beginning of your presentation (act one of the Speak Up System), when you grab your audience and get their attention. In segment one you introduce yourself. In segment two you introduce your topic. In segment three you promise your audience that by the end of the interaction they will have specific information, tools or capabilities to address a pain, fear or unfulfilled desire.

Heroic Achievement: Telling a story that reveals a highly desirable quality you possess. (Also referred to as "heroic achievement story.")

Heroic Achievement Formula: A way to tell a story so it reveals how you overcame conflict or struggles and delivered a successful result. To tell this type of story and make an audience feel lucky they've met you, you must: 1) set the scene and reveal the conditions; 2) create conflict using action words—build suspense; 3) resolve the conflict with maximum effectiveness and minimum cost; and 4) formally introduce the hero (you) and then broadcast the moral so the audience sees how you will relate to their problems.

Highlight + Hand Out: Content you briefly discuss with your audience and give them for later review or to share with others.

Ideal Leadoff Component: The best bit of content to get your audience engaged in your topic from the start of act three (your streamlined content and the cognitive-emotive impact of your contribution). (*See also* Four Dimensions of Decision-Making.)

Individuality: Being recognized and appreciated for your talent, philosophy or contribution. (*See also* universal business values.)

Instructions: Giving your audience clear and easy-to-follow directions that deliver the results and commitments you desire in an interaction. Repeat them twice to give players time to integrate what you are telling them to do. You must have everything they need on hand in order for them to follow your instructions.

Intangible Gifts: Opportunities to win or potentially enjoy something of value.

Interaction Style: The style of interaction during a meeting—persuasive, team, training or briefing—that is necessary to support the audience transformation or change in mind-set you desire. Each style uses specific content to transform an audience's resistance into compliance. (*See also* briefing-style meeting, Four Dimensions of Decision-Making, persuasive-style meeting, team-style meeting and training-style meeting.)

Interactions: Any meeting, presentation or conversation. Interactions are the second half of your personal equation of success.

Itinerary: Your calendar of actions and interactions that lead to the outcomes you desire.

Library of Success: A physical or mental library where you store the information, insights and other material about those topics you'll likely address in meetings, presentations and conversations. This enables you to quickly access everything you need to prepare yourself for any interaction.

Linked Interactions: Your plan for two or more consecutive meetings, presentations or conversations with an individual or organization, moving them toward a long-term outcome.

Listening Trap: Allowing other people to dominate you by talking on and on while you just listen. This takes you away from your goal and ultimately jeopardizes your potential for success.

Meeting Maps: A list of the content components used to transform your audience's mind-set from resistant to compliant. May also be used as an agenda for a meeting.

Milestones: Clear signs of significant progress along your path to success.

Misery Triggers: Unrelenting, intermittent or impending problems that cause *pain*, *fear* or *unfulfilled desire*. Out-of-control costs, negative publicity or an unexpected gain by your competitor are typical misery triggers. (*See also* pain, fear and unfulfilled desire.)

Model Speak Up Orchestration: The different tempos that typically maximize the impact of each component or section of content. (*See also* allegro, andante, presto, spirito, staccato and vivace.)

Nugget: An exclusive, time-sensitive or unusual fact that creates interest in an audience that may be indifferent to the topic.

Observability: Seeing others being effective with a product. (*See also* why-to-buys.)

Open Mind: A mind with no direction, which makes you a dumping ground for others' opinions, priorities and desires.

Outcome Maps: Written accounts of your business or career goals, or outcomes, and the milestones you must reach along the path to success.

Outcome Mind: Having a clear goal plus a map and timeline to get there. An outcome mind makes you a natural leader in an interaction since you know the direction you want it to go.

Over-Listening: Letting your audience take too much time to make a point and losing your opportunity to make your case.

Owls: Players who are wise, principled, philosophical and learned in many disciplines and topics. (*See also* player profiles and players.)

Pain: The state of mind when a person or organization suffers a significant loss or plunges into misfortune. This also occurs when something overlooked is suddenly needed, absent or difficult to get. (*See also* misery triggers.)

Peacocks: These players are flashy and attention grabbing, incredibly impatient with details and quick to give approval or deny permission. (*See also* player profiles and players.)

Peccadilloes: Petty and often offensive faults or flaws. (*See also* 3P soup.)

Personality: Distinctive, noticeable character traits. (*See also* 3P soup.)

Personalized Portfolio of Careers: The plan you create and implement so you continually take on more of the most satisfying work, jobs or business throughout your life.

Persuasive-Style Meeting: Changes your audience's mind-set from negative to positive and from bored or indifferent to enthusiastic.

Pivotal Questions: Showstoppers that change the direction of an interaction. These what if questions tie in to your audience's misery and use values to show them how to make a good decision. For example, Would it empower our managers and improve employee performance if everyone had one easy-to-read report? (*See also* showstoppers.)

Player Profiles: The personalities and interests of your players that you must accommodate so they lower their resistance to you. They are: ducks (followers), peacocks (big-idea folks), woodpeckers (those who poke holes and hammer you), owls (wise, long-term thinkers) and chicken littles (nervous micro-managers). (*See also* Four Dimensions of Decision-Making.)

Players: Individuals or organizations playing a substantial role in your success. They can accelerate or prevent your progress. Major players have the authority to say yes or no to things like promotions or funding. Minor players are those around you who may be unmotivated or difficult to manage and who can delay or derail your progress.

Pocket Topic Guide: A reference booklet available under Book Bonuses at www.NanceSpeaks.com that you fill with content components so you may quickly organize your thoughts before an interaction.

Preferences: Personal priorities and interests. (*See also* 3P soup.)

Presto: Fast; a rapid walking speed. Use when giving tips. (*See also* model speak up orchestration.)

Promise: Your guarantee that by the end of the interaction your audience will have something valuable that they can use to remedy a pain, fear or unfulfilled desire.

Proximate Outcome: The results and commitments you want from a particular individual interaction. You want a clear sign that the relationship has begun or deepened.

Relationship Map: A series of linked interactions that lead toward your desired outcome with each person or organization along your path.

Relationship Outcome: The long-term result or continuing benefits you plan to receive from working with a particular person or organization.

Relationship Scale: A measure of the balance or imbalance between what you give your audience versus what they are giving to you. During the interaction, you want to create an imbalance in their favor so that they feel compelled to give you what you want in your great closing.

Resistance and Compliance Scale: A way to assess your audience's current mind-set concerning the topic and result you desire in an upcoming interaction.

Rule of Reciprocity, The: A term in sociology that explains why people take turns. When you offer value beyond your audience's expectations, they feel indebted to you and want to give you something in return.

Satisfy: To delight your audience by delivering more than they expected.

Security: Feeling prepared and safe in the face of looming consequences. (*See also* universal business values.)

Showstoppers: Brief, powerful and memorable statements or questions that illustrate your insightful and trustworthy characteristics. Showstoppers usually focus on misery (pain, fear or unfulfilled desire) and touch on a solution that goes beyond the immediate problem and allows your audience to see their values in action.

Simplicity: Fast and easy to implement. (*See also* why-to-buys.)

Speak Up Star: What you become when you use the three-act Speak Up System regularly and experience the success that comes from driving interactions to your benefit and the benefit of your organization. You will enjoy a reputation for being perceptive, insightful, intelligent, trustworthy and central to the success of your team, department and organization.

Speak Up System: A powerful method of speaking that rapidly gets the results and commitments you desire in any meeting, presentation and conversation. It turns any resistance toward you or your proposal into enthusiastic compliance. The system uses three acts to organize and deliver content: 1) your great opening; 2) streamlined content; and 3) your great closing. As you deliver content in this format, you rapidly take your audience through five stages of transformation: 1) attention; 2) knowledge; 3) preference; 4) conviction; and 5) action. The Speak Up System is the backbone of your success any time you have five minutes or more with an audience.

Speak Up Time Split: Divides your presentation into the amount of time you should spend on each section: fifteen percent on act one, your great opening; seventy percent on act two, your streamlined content; and fifteen percent on act three, your great closing.

Speak Up: To express yourself in a powerful and persuasive way. Use words that drive others to take action exactly as you desire, accelerating your progress along the path to success. Speaking up to influence others is the greatest tool you have to reach your goals.

Speed of Benefit: Some immediate improvement. (*See also* why-to-buys.)

Spirito: Spirited. Use when interactivity or demonstrations are involved. (*See also* model speak up orchestration.)

Staccato: Separate; sounded in a short, detached manner. Helps register logic and insights. (*See also* model speak up orchestration.)

Startling Statistic: Numbers or percentages that relay a measurement of performance that can be credited to you or your team.

Sticky Decisions: The agreements and commitments that your audience makes that last after the interaction is over. Best achieved through your sharing content and facilitating audience experiences.

Strategic Advantage: Provides a real or perceived edge over others. (*See also* why-to-buys.)

Streamlined Content: The middle or content portion of your presentation (act two of the Speak Up System) when you give your audience the knowledge they need, the comparisons that create their preference for your proposal or point of view and the feeling of conviction that they must act now or risk losing out.

Success Story: An anecdote about the positive result achieved by another person or organization. It's especially effective when the story involves a high-profile person or organization.

Surprising Example or Analogy: Useful when you have to share complex or technical material. Use this to make a clear connection between something your audience already understands and what they are about to learn from you.

Sweetener: Something your audience did not expect but definitely wants. (*See also* extra gift, intangible gifts and tangible gifts.)

Symbolism: Has a greater meaning or a special connection. (*See also* why-to-buys.)

Tangible Gifts: Real property or intellectual property such as pens, software or gift certificates.

Team-Style Meeting: Changes your audience's mind-set from disconnected to unified and from self-centered to group goal oriented.

Time and Tempo/Style: In the Speak Up System, using your time most effectively means you typically spend fifteen percent on your great opening, seventy percent on your streamlined content and fifteen percent on your great closing. The delivery of each content component should vary in pace, volume and pitch to maximize its impact. For instance, difficult technical material necessitates your going slowly and steadily. A success story should be delivered in an upbeat manner. (*See also* Four Dimensions of Decision-Making and model speak up orchestration.)

Topic Meter: A method used to plot your audience's anticipated reaction to your topic. It measures their sensitivity, as well as your topic's significance and freshness. Their reaction could be flat, simmering, boiling or explosive. You want it to be hot, but not too hot.

Training-Style Meeting: Changes your audience's mind-set from deficient to proficient and from unsure to confident.

Transformation Channel: The five stages your audience must move through. It starts with your gaining their *attention* (stage one) in your great opening. Then via your streamlined content you help them develop *knowledge*, *preference* and *conviction* to take action (stages two, three and four). Finally, in your great closing, they follow your instructions and the *action* (stage five) and make the commitments you desire.

Trusted Advisor: Your desired role with any individual or organization, no matter what your job title actually is. After you use the Speak Up System regularly, you become a valued and respected resource in your organization or in your clients' organizations.

Ultimate Outcome: Your highest purpose or desire in life. Living the life of your dreams.

Unfulfilled Desire: The state of mind when a person or organization yearns for something that is all but unattainable. (*See also* misery triggers.)

Universal Business Values: Ideal qualities in life that people in business long for in their work, specifically: empowerment, security, vitality, creativity and individuality. (*See also* creativity, empowerment, individuality, security and vitality.)

Values Gap: The gulf between real-life situations and idealized ones. This is the source of most dissatisfaction and pain. You want yourself, your products, services and solutions to be seen as a bridge over that gap.

Values: The beliefs and aspirations that people hold up as ideal ways of living. These include peace of mind, freedom, love, joy, legacy, community, spirituality, security and family.

Vitality: Being healthy, strong and flexible, with the capacity to grow and compete. (*See also* universal business values.)

Vivace: Very spirited; bright; rapid. Ideal for leadoff components. (*See also* model speak up orchestration.)

Why-to-Buys: The seven reasons why people buy products, services and brands: compatibility, simplicity, speed of benefit, easy trial, observability, strategic advantage and symbolism. (*See also* compatibility, easy trial, observability, simplicity, speed of benefit, strategic advantage and symbolism.)

Woodpeckers: Players who are constantly poking holes in others' assertions. They are persistent, predictable and satisfied to do the same work over and over. (*See also* player profiles and players.)

For a wealth of information about training, visit www.NanceSpeaks.com. You may reach Nance by calling 1-888-GO NANCE or via e-mail at Nance@NanceRosen.com. Mail may be sent to Nance Rosen, PO Box 7816, Beverly Hills, CA 90212.